Harnessing Artificial intelligence for Unrivaled Cyber Security in the Digital Frontier

Repelling Threats, and Mastering the Future of Cybersecurity with Artificial Intelligence"

JAMES BRANDY

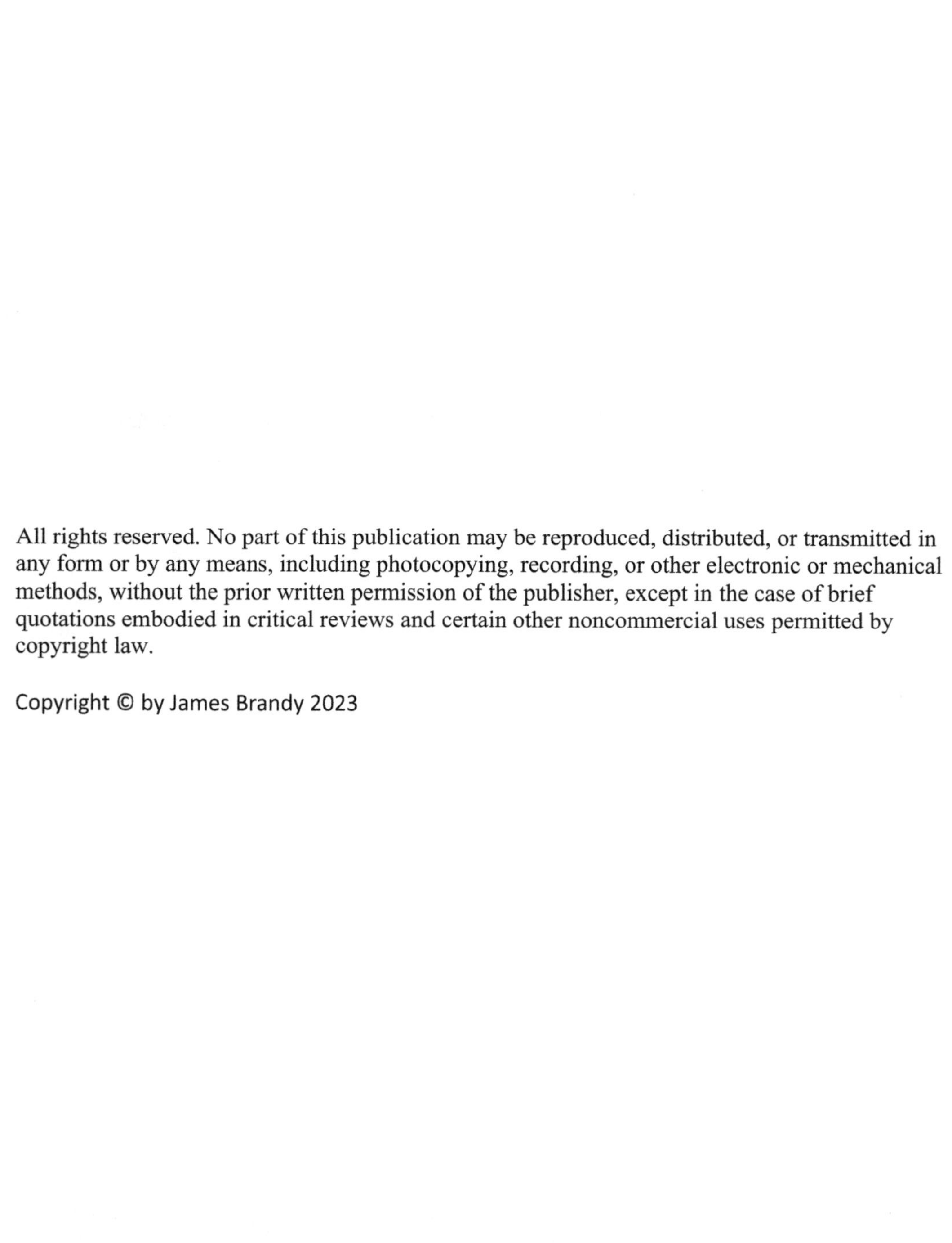

TABLE OF CONTENTS

INTRODUCTION

In an era defined by unprecedented connectivity and digital innovation, the landscape of cyber threats has evolved at an astonishing pace. The omnipresence of technology has brought about a paradigm shift, not only in the way we conduct business, communicate, and live our lives but also in the nature and sophistication of the threats that loom in the digital shadows.

"The Rise of Cyber Guard: Harnessing AI for Unrivaled Security in the Digital Frontier" delves into the heart of this dynamic landscape, where the battleground between cyber attackers and defenders is increasingly complex. As we witness the evolution of cyber threats, ranging from traditional malware to sophisticated nation-state-sponsored attacks, the imperative for a robust and adaptive cybersecurity strategy has never been more critical.

At the forefront of this defense is Artificial Intelligence (AI), a transformative force that has reshaped the cybersecurity paradigm. This book aims to unravel the intricate tapestry of cyber threats, providing insights into the historical context of their evolution and the pivotal role that AI plays in fortifying our digital defenses.

We embark on a journey that explores not only the vulnerabilities inherent in our interconnected world but also the revolutionary potential of AI to proactively detect, prevent, and respond to cyber threats. By understanding the intricacies of both the threat landscape and the AI technologies that combat them, readers will gain a comprehensive perspective on the contemporary challenges and opportunities in cybersecurity.

As we navigate through the pages of this book, we will unravel the symbiotic relationship between the evolution of cyber threats and the advancements in AI, paving the way for a future where our digital frontier is not just defended but fortified with intelligence and resilience. Welcome to "The Rise of Cyber Guard," where knowledge becomes the ultimate shield in the ongoing battle for digital security.

CHAPTER ONE

Foundations of Cybersecurity

In the ever-expanding digital landscape, where the heartbeat of global connectivity resonates with every click and keystroke, the imperative for robust cybersecurity has never been more pressing. This chapter serves as the cornerstone, laying the groundwork for our journey into the intricate realm of cybersecurity. We embark on a quest to understand the fundamental principles that underpin the defense mechanisms safeguarding our digital existence.

1.1 Understanding Cybersecurity Basics

To comprehend the essence of cybersecurity, one must first navigate the complex web of terminologies, concepts, and principles that define this domain. We begin with an exploration of the basic tenets — confidentiality, integrity, and availability that form the bedrock of cybersecurity. Delving into these core principles provides a lens through which we can analyze and fortify our digital defenses against an array of threats.

As we navigate this intellectual terrain, we explore the anatomy of cyber threats, ranging from the ubiquitous phishing attacks to the more sophisticated malware infiltrations. Understanding the adversary is key to constructing an effective defense, and this chapter elucidates the motivations, techniques, and tactics employed by cybercriminals.

1.2 Traditional Approaches and Limitations

Before the era of Artificial Intelligence revolutionized cybersecurity, defenders relied on traditional approaches to thwart digital threats. In this section, we delve into the historical evolution of cybersecurity practices, from the early days of firewalls and antivirus software to the challenges posed by the ever-expanding attack surface.

While traditional methodologies have played a crucial role in the defense playbook, they come with inherent limitations. We dissect the vulnerabilities and gaps that persist in these conventional approaches, shedding light on the need for a paradigm shift. This sets the stage for the transformative role that Artificial Intelligence assumes in augmenting our cybersecurity arsenal.

Join us in this exploration of the foundations of cybersecurity, where the building blocks of knowledge become the scaffold upon which we construct a resilient defense against the ever-evolving threats in the digital realm. As we journey through these pages, we equip ourselves with the understanding needed to navigate the complexities of cyberspace and pave the way for the intelligent guardianship of our digital future.

CHAPTER TWO

Traditional Approaches and Limitations

In the ever-evolving landscape of cybersecurity, understanding the roots of traditional approaches is crucial for building a solid foundation. As we delve into the historical perspective, we uncover the strengths and limitations that have shaped the cybersecurity landscape we know today.

2.1 The Evolution of Traditional Security Measures

Before the digital age, security primarily revolved around physical barriers and safeguards. However, as technology advanced and information became digitalized, traditional security models had to adapt. One of the earliest models, the perimeter defense approach, sought to create a fortified boundary around networks and systems. Firewalls and intrusion detection systems were deployed to monitor and control incoming and outgoing traffic. While effective to some extent, this model faced challenges as the concept of the network perimeter became increasingly porous.

2.2 Antivirus Software and Signature-based Detection

The rise of malicious software, or malware, prompted the development of antivirus solutions employing signature-based detection. These tools relied on a database of known malware signatures to identify and eliminate threats. While successful against known and well-established malware, this approach struggled with polymorphic and zero-day threats—malware that constantly changes its code or exploits vulnerabilities before they are officially discovered.

2.3 Limitations of Reactive Approaches

Traditional security approaches, including signature-based detection and perimeter defense, share a common limitation—they are reactive. In essence, they respond to known threats after an incident occurs. This reactive nature leaves organizations vulnerable to emerging and sophisticated attacks that exploit new vulnerabilities.

2.4 Vulnerabilities in Authentication Models

Authentication, a fundamental component of security, has seen its share of vulnerabilities in traditional models. Password-based authentication, widely used for decades, is prone to human errors, weak passwords, and susceptibility to brute-force attacks. Multi-factor authentication emerged as a step forward, but even this has its limitations, particularly in cases where users neglect or find workarounds for additional layers of security.

2.5 Challenges in Network Security

Network security traditionally relied on securing communication channels and enforcing access controls. While effective in many scenarios, these approaches faced challenges in the era of mobile devices, remote work, and the proliferation of Internet of Things (IoT) devices. The dynamic and diverse nature of modern networks requires more adaptive and comprehensive solutions.

2.6 The Need for a Paradigm Shift

As we reflect on the limitations of traditional approaches, it becomes evident that the ever-expanding attack surface and the rapid evolution of cyber threats demand a paradigm shift. Cybersecurity must move from a reactive stance to a proactive and adaptive posture. In the following chapters, we will explore the emerging technologies and strategies that form the foundation of modern cybersecurity, addressing the shortcomings of traditional models and providing a robust defense against the evolving threat landscape.

CHAPTER THREE

The Rise of AI in Cybersecurity

In this chapter, we plunge into the transformative realm where Artificial Intelligence emerges as the vanguard in our ongoing battle against cyber threats. As we navigate the intricate landscape of AI in cybersecurity, we explore three pillars that have reshaped the defense paradigm: Machine Learning, Deep Learning, and Natural Language Processing.

3.1 Machine Learning and Its Application

Machine Learning (ML) stands as the linchpin in the integration of AI into cybersecurity. This section peels back the layers of ML, unraveling its inner workings and the pivotal role it plays in bolstering our digital defenses. From supervised and unsupervised learning to reinforcement learning, we traverse the spectrum of ML techniques that empower systems to learn, adapt, and evolve in response to emerging threats.

Furthermore, we delve into real-world applications of ML in cybersecurity, ranging from anomaly detection and behavior analysis to predictive modeling. Through case studies and examples, we witness the tangible impact of ML algorithms in fortifying organizations against the dynamic landscape of cyber threats.

3.2 Deep Learning for Threat Detection

As cyber threats grow in complexity, traditional security measures face limitations in their ability to discern subtle patterns and anomalies. Deep Learning, a subset of ML, emerges as a game-changer. This section explores the architecture of neural networks, convolutional neural networks (CNNs), and recurrent neural networks (RNNs), unveiling their prowess in enhancing threat detection capabilities.

We examine how Deep Learning algorithms excel in discerning intricate patterns within vast datasets, offering a level of sophistication that was once unimaginable. From image recognition to behavioral analysis, Deep Learning algorithms become the digital sentinels that tirelessly scrutinize the digital landscape for any sign of malevolence.

3.3 Natural Language Processing in Security

The vast expanse of digital communication necessitates a nuanced understanding of language, and Natural Language Processing (NLP) emerges as a crucial facet of cybersecurity. In this section, we explore how NLP equips security systems with the ability to interpret, analyze, and respond to human language.

From identifying malicious intent in textual data to analyzing the intricacies of phishing attempts, NLP has become an indispensable tool in the cybersecurity arsenal. We unravel how machines comprehend and respond to language, paving the way for intelligent systems that can thwart linguistic-based cyber threats.

As we delve deeper into the amalgamation of AI and cybersecurity, this chapter serves as a compass, guiding us through the revolutionary technologies that redefine the boundaries of defense. Join us on this exploration of Machine Learning, Deep Learning, and Natural Language Processing, where the rise of AI becomes synonymous with the rise of a more intelligent and adaptive cybersecurity frontier.

In this chapter, we plunge into the transformative realm where Artificial Intelligence emerges as the vanguard in our ongoing battle against cyber threats. As we navigate the intricate landscape of AI in cybersecurity, we explore three pillars that have reshaped the defense paradigm: Machine Learning, Deep Learning, and Natural Language Processing.

3.1 Machine Learning and Its Application

Machine Learning (ML) stands as the linchpin in the integration of AI into cybersecurity. This section peels back the layers of ML, unraveling its inner workings and the pivotal role it plays in bolstering our digital defenses. From supervised and unsupervised learning to reinforcement learning, we traverse the spectrum of ML techniques that empower systems to learn, adapt, and evolve in response to emerging threats.

Furthermore, we delve into real-world applications of ML in cybersecurity, ranging from anomaly detection and behavior analysis to predictive modeling. Through case studies and examples, we witness the tangible impact of ML algorithms in fortifying organizations against the dynamic landscape of cyber threats.

3.2 Deep Learning for Threat Detection

As cyber threats grow in complexity, traditional security measures face limitations in their ability to discern subtle patterns and anomalies. Deep Learning, a subset of ML, emerges as a game-changer. This section explores the architecture of neural networks, convolutional neural networks (CNNs), and recurrent neural networks (RNNs), unveiling their prowess in enhancing threat detection capabilities.

We examine how Deep Learning algorithms excel in discerning intricate patterns within vast datasets, offering a level of sophistication that was once unimaginable. From image recognition to behavioral analysis, Deep Learning algorithms become the digital sentinels that tirelessly scrutinize the digital landscape for any sign of malevolence.

3.3 Natural Language Processing in Security

The vast expanse of digital communication necessitates a nuanced understanding of language, and Natural Language Processing (NLP) emerges as a crucial facet of cybersecurity. In this section, we explore how NLP equips security systems with the ability to interpret, analyze, and respond to human language.

From identifying malicious intent in textual data to analyzing the intricacies of phishing attempts, NLP has become an indispensable tool in the cybersecurity arsenal. We unravel how machines comprehend and respond to language, paving the way for intelligent systems that can thwart linguistic-based cyber threats.

As we delve deeper into the amalgamation of AI and cybersecurity, this chapter serves as a compass, guiding us through the revolutionary technologies that redefine the boundaries of defense. Join us on this exploration of Machine Learning, Deep Learning, and Natural Language Processing, where the rise of AI becomes synonymous with the rise of a more intelligent and adaptive cybersecurity frontier.

CHAPTER FIVE

Incident Response and Mitigation

In the dynamic world of cybersecurity, incidents are not a matter of "if" but "when." In this chapter, we delve into the critical realm of incident response and mitigation, exploring how Artificial Intelligence (AI) transforms the landscape of identifying, responding to, and mitigating cyber incidents. Our exploration encompasses three key facets: AI-powered incident Identification, Automated Incident Response Strategies, and the indispensable role of human collaboration in Crisis Management.

5.1 AI-Powered Incident Identification

The traditional methods of incident identification often rely on predefined patterns and signatures, leaving organizations vulnerable to novel and sophisticated threats. This section unveils the transformative capabilities of AI in enhancing the speed and accuracy of incident identification. We explore the role of machine learning algorithms in analyzing vast datasets to detect subtle anomalies, behavioral changes, and indicators of compromise that may elude conventional detection mechanisms.

Through real-world examples and case studies, we witness how AI-powered incident identification not only shortens the detection time but also minimizes false positives, allowing security teams to focus their efforts on genuine threats. As we navigate this landscape, we understand how the synergy between human expertise and AI intelligence becomes a force multiplier in the face of evolving cyber risks.

5.2 Automated Incident Response Strategies

Once an incident is identified, the ability to respond swiftly and effectively is paramount. This section delves into the realm of automated incident response, where AI-driven processes and workflows enable organizations to orchestrate a rapid and coordinated response. We explore the deployment of automated containment measures, threat eradication, and system recovery, reducing the impact and dwell time of cyber threats.

The chapter navigates through the intricacies of crafting automated incident response strategies, highlighting the importance of predefined playbooks, adaptive decision-making algorithms, and continuous refinement based on evolving threat landscapes. By harnessing the power of automation, organizations can significantly enhance their resilience against cyber incidents.

5.3 Human-AI Collaboration in Crisis Management

In the face of a cyber-crisis, the collaboration between human expertise and AI intelligence becomes paramount. This section explores how organizations can cultivate synergy between human analysts and AI systems, creating a cohesive crisis management framework. We delve into the roles and responsibilities of human responders, augmented by AI-driven insights, in making informed decisions during high-pressure situations.

Through case studies and best practices, we showcase the benefits of a collaborative approach, where AI provides real-time analysis and recommendations, empowering human responders to make timely and well-informed decisions. The chapter underscores the importance of training and communication protocols to ensure a seamless collaboration that maximizes the strengths of both human and artificial intelligence.

As we navigate the landscape of incident response and mitigation, this chapter unfolds the transformative power of AI in fortifying organizations against cyber threats. Join us on this exploration of AI-powered incident identification, automated response strategies, and the symbiotic collaboration between humans and AI in crisis management.

CHAPTER SIX

Threat Detection and Prevention

In the perpetual cat-and-mouse game of cybersecurity, the ability to detect and prevent threats is paramount. This chapter immerses us in the realm of advanced threat detection and prevention, where Artificial Intelligence (AI) stands as the guardian against an evolving array of cyber adversaries. Our exploration encompasses three pivotal aspects: Behavioral Analysis and Anomaly Detection, Predictive Modeling for Identifying Future Threats, and the implementation of Proactive Measures with AI.

6.1 Behavioral Analysis and Anomaly Detection

Traditional signature-based approaches fall short of identifying novel and sophisticated threats that often operate under the radar. This section unveils the power of behavioral analysis and anomaly detection, where AI algorithms scrutinize user and system behavior to detect deviations from the norm. By understanding what is "normal," AI systems can flag unusual activities indicative of potential threats.

We delve into the intricacies of behavioral analysis, exploring how AI models learn and adapt to the evolving patterns of user and system behavior. Through real-world scenarios and case studies, we witness how behavioral analysis becomes a cornerstone in identifying elusive threats that camouflage themselves within the noise of everyday digital activities.

6.2 Predictive Modeling for Identifying Future Threats

The landscape of cybersecurity extends beyond the present, and organizations must be prepared to anticipate and counter future threats. This section explores the realm of predictive modeling, where AI algorithms leverage historical data, threat intelligence, and machine learning to forecast potential future threats. By identifying emerging trends and vulnerabilities, organizations can proactively fortify their defenses.

We navigate through the methodologies of predictive modeling, shedding light on how AI-driven models extrapolate from past incidents to predict future attack vectors. The chapter underscores the importance of continuous learning and adaptation, as the threat landscape evolves, ensuring that organizations are ahead of the curve in their defense strategies.

6.3 Proactive Measures with AI

In the arms race between defenders and attackers, the ability to take proactive measures is a game-changer. This section elucidates how AI empowers organizations to adopt a proactive stance, actively hunting for potential threats rather than merely responding to known ones. We explore the deployment of AI-driven threat hunting, penetration testing, and vulnerability assessments to identify and mitigate risks before they can be exploited.

Through practical examples and use cases, we witness how proactive measures with AI not only enhance the overall security posture but also reduce the attack surface by closing vulnerabilities. The chapter concludes with insights into the importance of a holistic security strategy that integrates proactive measures into the organization's cybersecurity framework.

As we navigate through the intricacies of threat detection and prevention, this chapter unveils the transformative power of AI in fortifying organizations against both current and future cyber threats. Join us on this exploration of behavioral analysis, predictive modeling, and proactive measures as we delve deeper into the realm where AI becomes the vanguard of cybersecurity defense.

CHAPTER SEVEN

Advanced Incident Response and Mitigation

In the ever-evolving landscape of cybersecurity, incidents are not just disruptions but pivotal moments that define an organization's resilience. This chapter delves into the advanced aspects of incident response and mitigation, where the synergy between human expertise and Artificial Intelligence (AI) elevates crisis management to new heights. Our exploration covers three crucial dimensions: AI-Powered Incident Identification, Automated Incident Response Strategies, and the indispensable collaboration between humans and AI in crisis management.

7.1 AI-Powered Incident Identification: A Precision Instrument

As incidents become more sophisticated, the identification process requires a precision instrument capable of discerning subtle anomalies and emerging threats. This section reiterates the transformative impact of AI in incident identification, going beyond conventional methods. AI, with its ability to process vast datasets in real-time and recognize patterns, becomes the lens through which organizations can identify and classify incidents with unprecedented accuracy.

We delve into the advancements in AI algorithms that not only detect known threats but also analyze the behavioral nuances that may signal novel attacks. Through practical examples and case studies, we showcase how AI-powered incident identification not only reduces detection time but also enhances the precision of response efforts.

7.2 Automated Incident Response Strategies: Orchestrating a Rapid Defense

Once an incident is identified, the race against time begins. This section explores the realm of automated incident response, where AI-driven workflows and processes orchestrate a rapid and coordinated defense. We delve into the intricacies of crafting automated response strategies, from containment measures to threat eradication, all executed with speed and precision.

The chapter emphasizes the importance of predefined response playbooks, adaptive decision-making, and continuous refinement based on evolving threat landscapes. By harnessing the power of automation, organizations can significantly reduce the impact and recovery time in the face of cyber incidents.

7.3 Human-AI Collaboration in Crisis Management: The Power of Synergy

In the heat of a crisis, the collaboration between human responders and AI systems becomes a force multiplier. This section explores how organizations can foster a collaborative environment where human expertise and AI intelligence complement each other seamlessly. We delve into the roles and responsibilities of human responders augmented by AI-driven insights, showcasing the power of this symbiotic relationship in making informed decisions during high-pressure situations.

Through practical examples and best practices, we highlight the benefits of a collaborative approach. This collaboration not only enhances the effectiveness of crisis management but also leverages the strengths of both human and artificial intelligence to navigate the complexities of evolving cyber threats.

As we journey through the advanced realms of incident response and mitigation, this chapter illuminates the transformative role of AI in not only identifying and responding to incidents but also in fostering a collaborative crisis management framework. Join us on this exploration where AI becomes the linchpin in the quest for resilient and adaptive cybersecurity.

CHAPTER EIGHT

The Future Landscape of AI in Network Security

In this chapter, we venture into the horizon of AI in network security, exploring cutting-edge advancements and anticipating the future trends that will shape the digital defense landscape. Our exploration encompasses three key dimensions: Securing Networks with Intelligent Algorithms, Adaptive Defense Mechanisms, and Network Anomalies and Intrusion Detection.

8.1 Securing Networks with Intelligent Algorithms: A Quantum Leap

The evolution of intelligent algorithms continues to redefine the way we secure networks. In this section, we delve into the forefront of AI research, exploring emerging algorithms that push the boundaries of network security. From quantum-inspired computing to explainable AI, we examine how these innovations enhance the precision and adaptability of intelligent algorithms.

Through forward-looking case studies, we envision the application of advanced algorithms in securing next-generation networks. As we stand on the cusp of quantum computing, the chapter unravels the potential for AI to safeguard networks against threats that were once considered insurmountable.

8.2 Adaptive Defense Mechanisms: Orchestrating Cyber Resilience

As cyber threats become more sophisticated, the need for adaptive defense mechanisms intensifies. This section projects into the future, envisioning AI-driven defenses that autonomously adapt to the evolving threat landscape. We explore the integration of decentralized AI networks, enabling a collective defense approach where individual nodes learn and share threat intelligence in real time.

The chapter delves into the concept of predictive defenses, where AI anticipates and neutralizes threats before they materialize. We envision a future where autonomous response mechanisms not only mitigate risks but also actively hunt for potential vulnerabilities, ensuring a preemptive defense against emerging cyber threats.

8.3 Network Anomalies and Intrusion Detection: The Era of Predictive Security

The quest for proactive security measures intensifies as we peer into the future of network anomalies and intrusion detection. This section anticipates AI systems that not only detect deviations from the norm but also predict and prevent anomalies before they escalate into security incidents. We explore the integration of AI with quantum-resistant encryption, enhancing the confidentiality and integrity of network communications.

Through speculative scenarios, we envision AI-driven systems that fuse behavioral analytics with advanced threat intelligence, enabling predictive intrusion detection. The chapter foresees a future where AI becomes the intuitive guardian of networks, preemptively identifying and neutralizing threats in a continuous game of cyber chess.

As we conclude our exploration into the future landscape of AI in network security, this chapter serves as a beacon guiding us through the uncharted territories of technological advancement. Join us on this visionary journey where AI becomes the sentinel, adapting, predicting, and fortifying networks against the ever-evolving challenges in the digital domain.

CHAPTER NINE

Data Protection and Privacy

In an era where data is the lifeblood of digital interactions, safeguarding sensitive information and ensuring privacy are imperative. This chapter delves into the multifaceted domain of data protection and privacy, exploring key aspects such as Safeguarding Sensitive Information, GDPR and Regulatory Compliance, and Ethical Considerations in AI-driven Security.

9.1 Safeguarding Sensitive Information: The Fortification of Digital Assets

The digital landscape is rife with sensitive information, ranging from personal identifiers to corporate trade secrets. This section explores how organizations leverage AI to fortify their digital assets. We delve into encryption technologies, secure data storage methodologies, and AI-driven anomaly detection to safeguard sensitive information from unauthorized access.

Real-world case studies illuminate the effectiveness of AI in identifying and mitigating potential vulnerabilities in data protection strategies. As we navigate this landscape, we contemplate the evolving role of AI in enhancing the confidentiality, integrity, and availability of sensitive data.

9.2 GDPR and Regulatory Compliance: Navigating the Compliance Landscape

The regulatory landscape governing data protection underwent a seismic shift with the advent of the General Data Protection Regulation (GDPR). This section dissects the intricacies of GDPR and how AI becomes an instrumental tool in achieving and maintaining regulatory compliance.

We explore how AI technologies aid organizations in data mapping, consent management, and ensuring the right to be forgotten. Through insights into GDPR compliance frameworks, the chapter provides a roadmap for organizations to align their AI-driven security practices with the stringent regulatory requirements, ensuring the responsible and lawful handling of personal data.

9.3 Ethical Considerations in AI-driven Security: Balancing Innovation with Responsibility

As AI becomes deeply embedded in security practices, ethical considerations take center stage. This section navigates the ethical landscape of AI-driven security, examining the potential biases, transparency issues, and unintended consequences that may arise. We explore how organizations can uphold ethical standards in the development and deployment of AI technologies.

The chapter engages with the ethical considerations surrounding data collection, usage, and the impact of AI on privacy. Through case studies and ethical frameworks, we scrutinize the delicate balance between leveraging the innovative potential of AI in security and safeguarding the rights and privacy of individuals.

As we conclude this exploration into data protection and privacy, the chapter emphasizes the importance of striking a delicate equilibrium between technological advancement and ethical responsibility. Join us in contemplating the evolving landscape where AI becomes a cornerstone in the protection of sensitive information, compliance with regulations, and the ethical considerations that underpin responsible AI-driven security practices.

CHAPTER TEN

Cybersecurity in the Cloud Era

The proliferation of cloud computing has revolutionized the way organizations manage and deliver services. This chapter delves into the intricacies of cybersecurity in the cloud era, exploring key elements such as AI Solutions for Cloud Security, Securing Virtual Environments, and the Challenges and Opportunities inherent in Cloud-based Security.

10.1 AI Solutions for Cloud Security: Fortifying the Digital Skyline

The cloud, with its dynamic and scalable nature, presents both challenges and opportunities for cybersecurity. In this section, we explore how Artificial Intelligence (AI) solutions play a pivotal role in fortifying the digital skyline of cloud environments. From intelligent threat detection to adaptive access controls, AI has become a crucial ally in mitigating the evolving risks associated with cloud-based infrastructures.

We delve into the AI-driven tools and technologies that organizations employ to secure their cloud assets. Through real-world examples, we witness how AI enhances the resilience of cloud security by continuously learning, adapting, and responding to the ever-changing threat landscape.

10.2 Securing Virtual Environments: Navigating the Cloud Landscape

Virtualization technologies have become integral to the cloud ecosystem, introducing a new dimension to cybersecurity. This section explores the security considerations inherent in securing virtual environments within the cloud. We unravel the intricacies of network segmentation, hypervisor security, and the role of AI in ensuring the integrity and isolation of virtual workloads.

The chapter navigates through the challenges and best practices of securing virtualized infrastructure, providing insights into the convergence of AI-driven security measures with virtualization technologies. As organizations transition to cloud-native architectures, securing virtual environments becomes a cornerstone in the defense against cyber threats.

10.3 Challenges and Opportunities in Cloud-based Security: A Dynamic Landscape

The cloud era brings forth a dynamic landscape filled with both challenges and opportunities for cybersecurity practitioners. This section explores the multifaceted nature of cloud-based security, dissecting the challenges posed by shared responsibility models, data sovereignty concerns, and the complex interplay of security controls within cloud environments.

Simultaneously, we uncover the opportunities that arise from the flexibility and scalability offered by cloud platforms. We delve into how organizations can leverage AI-driven tools to automate security workflows, enforce compliance, and proactively identify and remediate vulnerabilities in the cloud.

As we conclude our exploration of cybersecurity in the cloud era, this chapter serves as a guide through the ever-evolving landscape of cloud-based security. Join us on this journey where AI solutions become the guardians of the cloud, securing virtual environments and navigating the challenges and opportunities presented by the dynamic nature of the digital sky.

As blockchain and edge computing. The chapter envisions a future where intelligent defenses are not only proactive but also self-learning, adapting in real time to the ever-changing tactics of cyber adversaries.

11.2 Emerging Threats and Countermeasures: Anticipating the Unseen

The future landscape of cybersecurity will undoubtedly be marked by new and sophisticated threats. In this section, we explore the emerging threats that organizations are likely to face and the countermeasures that will be essential for resilience. From AI-driven cyber-physical attacks to threats targeting decentralized technologies, we navigate through the evolving tactics and techniques employed by cyber adversaries.

We delve into the role of threat intelligence platforms, collaboration frameworks, and adaptive defense mechanisms as essential elements in countering emerging threats. The chapter envisions a future where organizations leverage AI not only to defend against known threats but also to anticipate and neutralize threats before they materialize.

11.3 Ethical and Policy Implications: Navigating the Digital Ethics Terrain

As the capabilities of cybersecurity technologies expand, ethical considerations and policy frameworks become paramount. This section examines the ethical implications of AI-driven cybersecurity practices, addressing issues of transparency, bias, and accountability. We explore how organizations can balance innovation with responsible AI deployment, ensuring that cybersecurity practices adhere to ethical standards.

The chapter also navigates the evolving policy landscape, including international collaboration efforts, cyber insurance frameworks, and regulatory developments. We anticipate a future where ethical considerations and policy frameworks play a pivotal role in shaping the norms and practices of cybersecurity on a global scale.

As we conclude this journey into the future landscape of cybersecurity, this chapter serves as a compass, guiding us through the uncharted territories where technology, threats, and ethical considerations converge. Join us in envisioning a future where advancements in AI technology, proactive countermeasures, and ethical practices collectively define the resilient and responsible cybersecurity practices of tomorrow.

CHAPTER TWELVE

Case Studies and Success Stories

In this final chapter, we embark on a journey through real-world examples that showcase the transformative impact of AI in the field of cybersecurity. Drawing from diverse industries and organizations, we explore how AI technologies have been implemented to tackle cyber threats. Along the way, we extract valuable lessons learned from these implementations, offering insights into the challenges faced, the strategies employed, and the success stories that have unfolded.

12.1 Real-world Examples of AI in Action

This section brings the theoretical into the tangible by examining real-world cases where AI has been deployed to enhance cybersecurity. From large enterprises to small businesses, we delve into the specifics of AI applications that have demonstrated efficacy in threat detection, incident response, and overall security posture.

Case studies will span a spectrum of scenarios, including the proactive use of AI in identifying and thwarting potential threats, the integration of AI into existing security frameworks, and the application of AI in response to specific cyber incidents. By exploring these real-world examples, readers gain a nuanced understanding of the practical impact and versatility of AI technologies in diverse cybersecurity contexts.

12.2 Lessons Learned from Implementations

The implementation of AI in cybersecurity is not without its challenges, and this section distills valuable lessons from the front lines. We explore the experiences of organizations that have pioneered AI-driven security initiatives, uncovering the hurdles faced and the strategies employed to overcome them.

The lessons learned encompass technical considerations, organizational readiness, and the importance of human-AI collaboration. We also delve into the iterative nature of AI implementations, emphasizing the need for continuous learning and adaptation to stay ahead of evolving cyber threats.

As we conclude our exploration of case studies, we reflect on the collective wisdom gained from these real-world implementations. The chapter aims to provide a guidepost for organizations embarking on their AI-driven cybersecurity journey, offering insights that can inform their strategies, mitigate challenges, and maximize the benefits of AI technologies.

In closing, this chapter celebrates the success stories born out of the synergy between AI and cybersecurity. From the battlefield of digital threats to the fortifications of resilient defense, these case studies stand as beacons, illuminating the path toward a more secure and adaptive future. Through their stories, we glean not only the achievements of today but also the inspiration for the continued evolution of cybersecurity in the years to come.

CHAPTER THIRTEEN

Preparing for the Cybersecurity Revolution

In this concluding chapter, we shift our focus to the future, exploring the essential elements for preparing individuals and organizations for the ongoing revolution in cybersecurity. From the skillsets required for tomorrow's cybersecurity professionals to strategies for navigating the evolving threat landscape and the importance of continuous learning, this chapter serves as a guidepost for embracing and thriving in the cybersecurity revolution.

13.1 Skill Sets for Tomorrow's Cybersecurity Professionals

The evolution of cybersecurity demands a corresponding evolution in the skillsets of professionals safeguarding digital landscapes. This section dissects the key skills and competencies that will be crucial for tomorrow's cybersecurity professionals. From expertise in AI and machine learning to a deep understanding of cloud security and cryptography, we delve into the multifaceted skill sets required to tackle the diverse and sophisticated challenges on the horizon.

Furthermore, we explore the importance of soft skills, such as communication, adaptability, and critical thinking, which are increasingly becoming indispensable in the collaborative and fast-paced world of cybersecurity. By understanding and cultivating these skill sets, aspiring and seasoned cybersecurity professionals alike can position themselves as invaluable assets in the digital defense ecosystem.

13.2 Navigating the Evolving Threat Landscape

As the threat landscape continues to evolve, organizations and individuals must develop strategies to navigate the complexities of the digital frontier. This section explores proactive approaches for anticipating and mitigating emerging threats. We delve into threat intelligence frameworks, collaborative information-sharing platforms, and the integration of AI-driven tools to bolster defense mechanisms.

Case studies and practical examples illuminate how organizations can stay ahead of cyber adversaries by understanding their tactics, techniques, and procedures. The chapter emphasizes the importance of threat hunting, vulnerability assessments, and incident response planning as integral components of a robust cybersecurity strategy.

13.3 Continuous Learning in the Digital Frontier

In the dynamic world of cybersecurity, where threats evolve at an unprecedented pace, the concept of continuous learning becomes paramount. This section underscores the need for professionals to embrace a mindset of perpetual learning. We explore avenues for staying updated on the latest technologies, threat vectors, and security best practices.

From industry certifications and online courses to participation in cybersecurity communities and conferences, we unravel the myriad opportunities for continuous education. The chapter also addresses the importance of fostering a culture of learning within organizations, where employees are encouraged to expand their knowledge and skills to collectively fortify the cybersecurity posture.

As we conclude this exploration into preparing for the cybersecurity revolution, this chapter serves as a call to action. Whether you are a seasoned professional or an aspiring cybersecurity enthusiast, the journey ahead demands a commitment to continuous learning, the cultivation of diverse skill sets, and an unwavering resolve to navigate the evolving threat landscape. Through these endeavors, individuals and organizations can not only adapt to the cybersecurity revolution but also actively shape its trajectory, ensuring a secure and resilient digital future.

In the pages of this book, we embarked on a comprehensive exploration of the multifaceted realm of cybersecurity, from its foundational principles to the cutting-edge innovations shaping its future. As we draw this journey to a close, let's recap the key insights and consider the uncharted horizons that lie ahead in the ever-evolving landscape of cybersecurity.

Recap of Key Insights:

Foundations of Cybersecurity: We began by laying the groundwork, and understanding the foundational principles of cybersecurity, including risk management, encryption, and access controls. These fundamentals provide the bedrock upon which resilient cybersecurity practices are built.

The Role of Artificial Intelligence: AI emerged as a transformative force, revolutionizing the way organizations defend against cyber threats. From intelligent threat detection to automated incident response, AI has become a linchpin in the digital defense arsenal.

Incident Response and Mitigation: Chapters delved into the crucial aspects of incident response, emphasizing the importance of AI-powered incident identification, automated response strategies, and the collaboration between humans and AI in crisis management.

Threat Detection and Prevention: We explored advanced techniques in threat detection and prevention, focusing on behavioral analysis, predictive modeling, and proactive measures empowered by AI. These strategies ensure a proactive defense against evolving cyber threats.

Network Security in the Cloud Era: With the advent of cloud computing, we navigated the challenges and opportunities in securing virtual environments. AI solutions and adaptive defense mechanisms became essential in fortifying the digital sky in the cloud era.

Data Protection and Privacy: Ethical considerations took center stage as we explored data protection and privacy in the digital landscape. GDPR compliance, safeguarding sensitive information, and navigating ethical terrain became imperative in the era of big data.

The Future Landscape of Cybersecurity: Looking forward, we envisioned a future shaped by advancements in AI technology, the emergence of new threats, and the ethical and policy implications that will define cybersecurity practices globally.

Case Studies and Success Stories: Real-world examples showcased the practical impact of AI in action, offering insights into successful implementations and the lessons learned from the front lines of cybersecurity.

Preparing for the Cybersecurity Revolution: The concluding chapters provided a roadmap for individuals and organizations to prepare for the ongoing revolution in cybersecurity. This involved developing the right skillsets, navigating the evolving threat landscape, and embracing continuous learning as a cornerstone of resilience.

Looking Ahead: The Uncharted Horizons of Cybersecurity

As we gaze into the future, the horizons of cybersecurity remain both promising and challenging. The integration of AI technologies will continue to evolve, presenting new opportunities for innovation and defense. The threat landscape will undoubtedly morph, necessitating adaptive strategies and collaboration across industries and borders.

Crucially, the uncharted horizons call for a workforce equipped with diverse skills, a commitment to continuous learning, and a profound ethical awareness. The cybersecurity revolution demands not only technological prowess but also a collective dedication to safeguarding the digital realm responsibly and ethically.

In conclusion, the journey through the pages of this book is just the beginning. As we venture into the uncharted horizons of cybersecurity, let us approach the challenges with resilience, curiosity, and a commitment to shaping a secure digital future for generations to come. The cybersecurity revolution is not a destination but an ongoing journey, and the path forward holds both the excitement of discovery and the responsibility of stewardship in the digital age.

CONCLUSIONS

Foundations of Cybersecurity: We began by laying the groundwork, and understanding the foundational principles of cybersecurity, including risk management, encryption, and access controls. These fundamentals provide the bedrock upon which resilient cybersecurity practices are built.

The Role of Artificial Intelligence: AI emerged as a transformative force, revolutionizing the way organizations defend against cyber threats. From intelligent threat detection to automated incident response, AI has become a linchpin in the digital defense arsenal.

Incident Response and Mitigation: Chapters delved into the crucial aspects of incident response, emphasizing the importance of AI-powered incident identification, automated response strategies, and the collaboration between humans and AI in crisis management.

Threat Detection and Prevention: We explored advanced techniques in threat detection and prevention, focusing on behavioral analysis, predictive modeling, and proactive measures empowered by AI. These strategies ensure a proactive defense against evolving cyber threats.

Network Security in the Cloud Era: With the advent of cloud computing, we navigated the challenges and opportunities in securing virtual environments. AI solutions and adaptive defense mechanisms became essential in fortifying the digital sky in the cloud era.

Data Protection and Privacy: Ethical considerations took center stage as we explored data protection and privacy in the digital landscape. GDPR compliance, safeguarding sensitive information, and navigating ethical terrain became imperative in the era of big data.

The Future Landscape of Cybersecurity: Looking forward, we envisioned a future shaped by advancements in AI technology, the emergence of new threats, and the ethical and policy implications that will define cybersecurity practices globally.

Case Studies and Success Stories: Real-world examples showcased the practical impact of AI in action, offering insights into successful implementations and the lessons learned from the front lines of cybersecurity.

Preparing for the Cybersecurity Revolution: The concluding chapters provided a roadmap for individuals and organizations to prepare for the ongoing revolution in cybersecurity. This involved developing the right skillsets, navigating the evolving threat landscape, and embracing continuous learning as a cornerstone of resilience.

Looking Ahead: The Uncharted Horizons of Cybersecurity

As we gaze into the future, the horizons of cybersecurity remain both promising and challenging. The integration of AI technologies will continue to evolve, presenting new opportunities for innovation and defense. The threat landscape will undoubtedly morph, necessitating adaptive strategies and collaboration across industries and borders.

Crucially, the uncharted horizons call for a workforce equipped with diverse skills, a commitment to continuous learning, and a profound ethical awareness. The cybersecurity revolution demands not only technological prowess but also a collective dedication to safeguarding the digital realm responsibly and ethically.

In conclusion, the journey through the pages of this book is just the beginning. As we venture into the uncharted horizons of cybersecurity, let us approach the challenges with resilience, curiosity, and a commitment to shaping a secure digital future for generations to come. The cybersecurity revolution is not a destination but an ongoing journey, and the path forward holds both the excitement of discovery and the responsibility of stewardship in the digital age.

Preparing for the Cybersecurity Revolution: The concluding chapters provided a roadmap for individuals and organizations to prepare for the ongoing revolution in cybersecurity. This involved developing the right skillsets, navigating the evolving threat landscape, and embracing continuous learning as a cornerstone of resilience.

Looking Ahead: The Uncharted Horizons of Cybersecurity

As we gaze into the future, the horizons of cybersecurity remain both promising and challenging. The integration of AI technologies will continue to evolve, presenting new opportunities for innovation and defense. The threat landscape will undoubtedly morph, necessitating adaptive strategies and collaboration across industries and borders.

Crucially, the uncharted horizons call for a workforce equipped with diverse skills, a commitment to continuous learning, and a profound ethical awareness. The cybersecurity revolution demands not only technological prowess but also a collective dedication to safeguarding the digital realm responsibly and ethically.

In conclusion, the journey through the pages of this book is just the beginning. As we venture into the uncharted horizons of cybersecurity, let us approach the challenges with resilience, curiosity, and a commitment to shaping a secure digital future for generations to come. The cybersecurity revolution is not a destination but an ongoing journey, and the path forward holds both the excitement of discovery and the responsibility of stewardship in the digital age.